An Unexpected Courtesy

the poetry of

ayaz daryl nielsen

Cyberwit.net
HIG 45 Kaushambi Kunj, Kalindipuram
Allahabad - 211011 (U.P.) India
http://www.cyberwit.net
Tel: +(91) 9415091004
E-mail: info@cyberwit.net

My deepest appreciation for the publications, print and online, where these poems first appeared: Barbaric Yawp, The Big Windows Review (Washtenaw Community College, Michigan), Cheap Seats, Cholla Needles Arts and Literary Library, Cyberwit, DASH Literary Journal (CSU-Fullerton), Episteme (Bharat College of Arts and Commerce, India), Fire, FreeXpresSion (Australia), HazMat, Kind of a Hurricane Press, Lalitamba, Lilliput Review, Lynx, Magnapoets, Montucky Review, multi-verse journal, Verse News, Northern Stars Magazine, Prolific Press Publications, Scars Publications, SciFaiKuest, SHAMROCK (Irish Haiku Society), SHEMOM, STAR*LINE, Trajectory Journal, Valley MicroPress (New Zealand), Verse Wrights, Verse Wisconsin, Whispers in the Wind, Wild Violet, and, Yellow Mama!

for Judith

our big old bookcase
even the empty spaces
a certain kindness

it takes some
    hocus-pocus
to steer this
    mumbo-jumbo

as far as tonight
come, darling, and let's just
surrender to us

cousins

past sinning,
mentors for my
current sins:
never alone
nor without
excuses
my pleasures are
first cousins: perky,
observant,
and always
ready to engage

no, morning breeze
you cannot have
her lingering scent

someone sighs outside
my open window— yes!
someone sighing!
morning light touching
a dark and familiar dream
as if forgiving

you, I
  even in silence
    everything

this strange swoop of thoughts
a poem with its kept secrets
suddenly opens

Last scene in the rearview mirror
                Watching from the front porch
                arms firmly crossed and her jacket
            zipped from bottom to buttoned collar
              As she sags against the doorway,
              I lightly touch the brake…
              She steps inside and closes the door.
                There are dry leaves everywhere
            on this high plains road…
              I push on the accelerator

An Unexpected Courtesy

evening meditation
    crickets, cicada and
        the Heart Sutra

bristlecone pine
    older than
        our religions

grinning about
all the gossip- -
we earned it

her new Crosstrek…
    does the cruise control
        know the way
            to my bedroom?

An Unexpected Courtesy

East Texas

blue-tailed salamanders
everywhere- - one in
the living room

The nights, long, the days,
cold, the meadow buried
under snowbanks. Broken
tree limbs sag beside our
roof's multi-tipped
icicles. Sandhill cranes
and wild geese left months
ago, the black bear, deep
asleep. Another subzero
wind from above the tree line.
Red-tail fox, in their den,
the mule deer, hiding among
ponderosa and leafless aspen.
The secondhand ticks
toward midnight, this long
year, ending, a new year will
begin. Here, beside our
warm fire, you gently
place your lips
upon mine.

the woodland midwife

green leaves and
almond-sized raindrops
a turquoise sky and
a lukewarm wind
her embroidery loom
of lastingness

seeping thorough
the moonlight
cicadas, chanting

Beloved

she asks with her eyes
if I love
in silence

this fool
says "yes"

she asks with her tears
can you love in silence

I, so foolish,
so grateful

silent
  within
    our embrace

a poem's resonance
unfinished exuberance
yes! writing again!

my happiness and how it came about

"and," she stated, "it's
time you settled down"
immediately, us,
eyeball-to-eyeball,
as she commands, "and
you're settling down with me"
and we've been happily
married ever since

An Unexpected Courtesy

oh, you falling rain
tell us why frogs sing at night
and everything else

intense restlessness
this quaking quickening from
an unwritten poem

a poem's resonance
unfinished exuberance
yes! writing again!

working on poems
un-encountered aliens
to be acknowledged

as I leave
snowdrops melting
on the warm windshield
a good-bye to you, too!

merry-go-round

well, the world
and all it's things
just keep on turning-
every now and then,
though, I step off
and take a break

fingers intertwined
hearts' inner eyes wide open
this oneness of us

a leviathan
begrudging the morning light…
I go back to sleep

Ty and Janet

Ty, little doggy with
blue-tinted glasses
a wrap around his neck
and a small coat
Janet, dressed the same
on the other end
of the leash

buttercup blossoms
choosing their sunlit angles
seeking the poetic

moments in Spring rain
quiet, private, sensual
touch, taste and scent
of re-birthing
a poem's resonance
an unfurled exuberance
love's testimony

An Unexpected Courtesy

fireflies   a forgotten dream

massive tree at
the western edge of
this quiet, goose-covered lake,
how I love thee
I've been am your green leaves,
your floating dry leaves,
have been/am the air you breathe,
the sun of your existence
the changes in our growth,
the grip of your roots
massive tree, I am you,
as you are me
and you, I, in love as
one holy presence
nurturing ourselves
and all the I's around us

train whistle
between
raindrops

grandma, singing
as she makes
breakfast for forty

alongside the county road
a saddled horse galloping
in one stirrup
an empty boot
lightning so bright
street-lights stutter

An Unexpected Courtesy

hundreds, yes, hundreds of geese
circling overhead,
spiraling down to the
lake I stand beside
no goose is alone
a few belated couples,
sometimes a quartet,
pass by after all the others- -
and I think of the woman
on the bridge that linked
the two buildings of
a library together,
watching geese float by
from underneath the bridge
as I pause, and watch beside her,
she turns to me, saying,
'geese mate for life, and when
a hunter shoots one of them,
the other mourns forever"
and she cries, and I
wipe away my own tears
and, thinking of it again, I shed
a matching pair of tears

poems
pathways for our
way home

oh, grandfather raven!
here you are, with us
for another season!
please, spread your wings
beyond the melting snow
and share the hidden tales!

esoteric studies while
seated at my shrine
outside the window,
two crows chuckling

a long flight of geese
holding my breath as they pass…
yesterday's, leaving

shimmers on the lake
placing one within my heart
taking it home for her

Three Wooden Trunks

Wooden trunks in the shed
decades of mice, owl and
pigeon droppings, of webs
thick with insect husks,
dirt and small feathers,
of sleepy feral cats we've
always fed lying on old
wool blankets... the uncle
who never came home
from one of those wars.

my dog, peeing
on the neighbor's
new boots

mossy steps
across a brook -
the lives of rocks

contemplating
the essence
of Holy Spirit…
an evening breeze
filled with
cottonwood seeds

An Unexpected Courtesy

Judith

beyond our cabin window
late evening snow falls

lingering beside your
delicious softness

I fill our empty glasses
with fine wine

tasting morning, falling snow,
sauvignon blanc,
and us

mind full friends

speak easily
openly words
of like minds
we'll caress their
undulating
movements
together
unveiling
the Beloved's
oneness

gibbous moon unfinished poems

All we have
is the moment–
here comes another
Let's name this one
"two people in love'

standing on a tree
stump beside the
old logging road…
from what depths
these tears?

chinook wind
the roof is gone
but the house is warm

the opera's best part
my wife's hand
upon my thigh

Alabama truck stop
different accents but
the same laughter

nervous as she
presents her poetry—
the slight quiver
enhances
a low-cut blouse

frogs!
the frogs of Spring!
oh, sacred croaking!
after the funeral
giving the suit I wore
to Good Will

old iron bed frame
the lover my pillows
gossip about

evening meditation
Avalokiteœvara's
cricket sutra

my old dog sprawls
across the open docrway
neither in nor out

An Unexpected Courtesy

Chaco Canyon petroglyphs

evening rainbow and moonbeams
moon shadows and moon dancers
cicada's love songs

four flute players
four spiral dancers
limitless design

lichen silver
embracing
ancestor bear

Taps, echoing…
military graveyard
again… again…
again…

Beginnings

Halfway to poetry
Halfway to an ending
and I hear the call
of a new beginning…

Can you meet me here,
halfway? Can you wait
until I arrive at
where we could begin?…

Will you wait for me?

An Unexpected Courtesy

when we met
I knew space within my heart
had to expand

rugged mountain path
stopping often to
catch my breath
and the poetry
within a moment

the Heartland Cafe…
my parents and I
often went there

autumn chore…
moving caterpillars
from the bike path